W9-AJT-012
3 1160 00545 1120

INLINE SKATING

First American edition published in 2004
by LernerSports

This book is available in two editions:
Library binding by LernerSports
Soft cover by First Avenue Editions
Imprints of Lerner Publishing Group
241 First Avenue North
Minneapolis, MN 55401 U.S.A.

Website address: www.lernerbooks.com

Designed and produced by:
David West Children's Books
7 Princeton Court
55 Felsham Road
London, England

Designer: Gary Jeffrey
Editor: James Pickering
Picture Research: Carlotta Cooper

Library of Congress Cataloging-in-Publication Data

Glidewell, Steve.
Inline skating / by Steve Glidewell.—1st American ed.
p. cm. — (Extreme Sports)
Includes index.
Summary: Discusses the history, skates, safety, techniques, tricks, and styles—including aggressive—of inline skating.
ISBN: 0–8225–1244–0 (lib. bdg.)
ISBN: 0–8225–1194–0 (pbk.)
1. In-line skating—Juvenile literature. [1. In-line skating. 2. Extreme Sports.] I. Title: In line skating. II. Title. III. Extreme Sports (Minneapolis, Minn.)
GV859.73.G55 2004
796.21—dc21 2002155400

Bound in the United States of America
1 2 3 4 5 6 – OS – 09 08 07 06 05 04

PHOTO CREDITS :
Abbreviations: t-top, m-middle, b-bottom, r-right, l-left, c-center.

Front cover - Corbis Images. 3, 15b, 16t, 18-19, 19, 20t, 21 both, 22b, 28br, 28-29, 29bl - Chris Hallam. 4-5, 24-25b, 27l - Adam Kola. 5, 23l, 25l - Buzz Pictures. 6t - Karen Augusta, www.antique-fashion.com. 6b, 7t - Hulton Archive. 7b - The Kobal Collection / JVC / TV Tokyo / GAGA. 8l, 9t, 10br, 11mr & b, 12-13, 16b, 18, 20b, 22, 24t & m, 26b - Steve Glidewell. 8b - USD Skates. 9bl - Able Hardware. 9br - Salomon. 13m, 30 - Corbis Images. 26t, 27tr, 29tr - Gilles Alburge. 28bl, 29ml - Pictures Courtesy of Aggressive.com. 29br - Jess Dyrenforth / Rollerblade.

An explanation of difficult words can be found in the glossary on page 31.

extreme sports

INLINE SKATING

Steve Glidewell

CONTENTS

STREET SKATING
A street skater slides, or "grinds," his skates down a handrail. All skaters must balance the risks of a stunt against their skill.

Introduction

Inline skating is probably the most popular extreme sport in the world. For some people, it's a great form of exercise. For more ambitious, or "aggressive," skaters, it's the thrill of overcoming all the obstacles that cities and skateparks can offer. A lucky few can even earn a living from the sport, demonstrating their skills in thrilling competitions.

GRAB
A skater performs a "grab," clutching his skates in midair.

WARNING!

INLINE SKATING CAN BE AN **EXTREMELY DANGEROUS** SPORT. DO NOT ATTEMPT ANY MOVES **BEYOND YOUR ABILITIES** AND ALWAYS WEAR THE APPROPRIATE SAFETY EQUIPMENT.

Skating on ice has been popular for centuries. But before the invention of ice rinks, skating was governed by the weather. People wanted to be able to skate on dry land year-round.

EARLY QUADS
The wheels of Plimpton's skates were made of wood. They were supported by rubber springs.

The Need for Speed

The first known roller skates were invented in the mid-1700s. For the next century, all skates were based on this design. In 1819 the French started making skates with three wheels in a line. It was difficult to turn or skate backward on these skates. In 1863 James Plimpton revolutionized skating by putting two pairs of wheels on a skate, side by side. Called quad skates, these skates were much easier to control. The four-wheeled skate soon dominated the industry.

CUSHIONING THE BLOW
Before the invention of knee pads and wrist guards, people still needed safety gear and used homemade equipment!

ROLLER GANGS

Because there were so few cars, the street was a safer place to play during the early 1900s. But nobody attempted any of the modern stunts.

PRAYER OF THE ROLLERBOYS

The movie business eventually latched on to the popularity of skating. The 1991 film *Prayer of the Rollerboys* was a science fiction adventure about a gang of teenage skaters.

Roller skating grew more popular during the 1900s. In the 1970s, advances in technology changed skating from a hobby into a true sport.

1819 INLINE
The very first skates had their wheels in a row, just like modern inline skates.

Dancing Days

The invention of polyurethane (hard plastic) wheels changed roller skates forever. These wheels were tough. They provided a smooth ride with minimum friction. Roller-discos opened up everywhere. Sleek dance floors allowed skaters to practice their moves to the latest music. In 1979 two Minnesota brothers, Scott and Brennan Olson, found an antique pair of inline skates. They decided to mimic the design and add polyurethane wheels. Their Rollerblade company soon became a byword for inline skating.

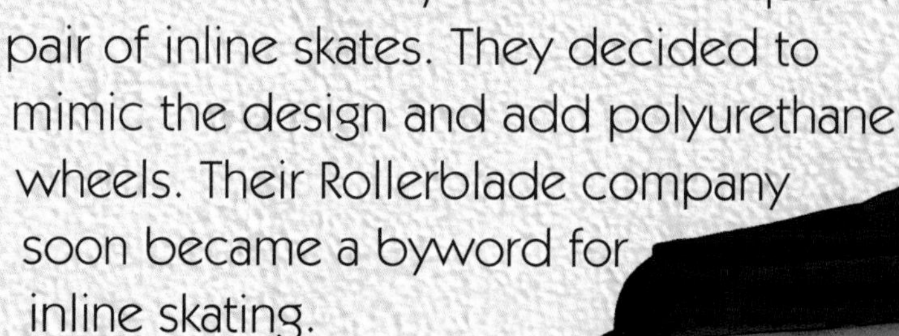

WHEELS
A wheel's hardness is measured on the durometer scale. The higher the durometer reading, the better the wheel is for grinding.

Wheel Setup

When skaters first thought about grinding walls and ledges, they took the second and third wheels out of their frames. They replaced them with small skateboard wheels. Special grind wheels started to be made. They were smaller and very hard.

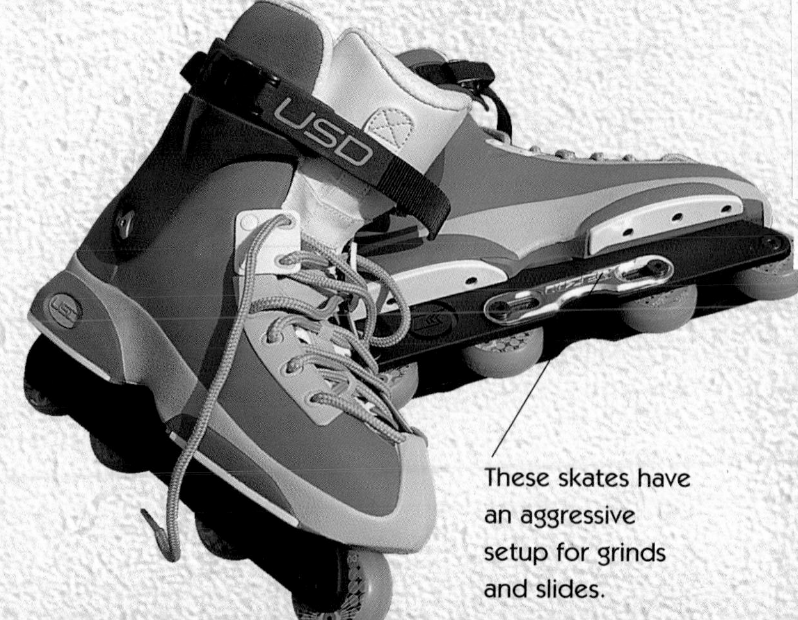

These skates have an aggressive setup for grinds and slides.

GUIDE #1

BOOTS

There are three main types of boots.

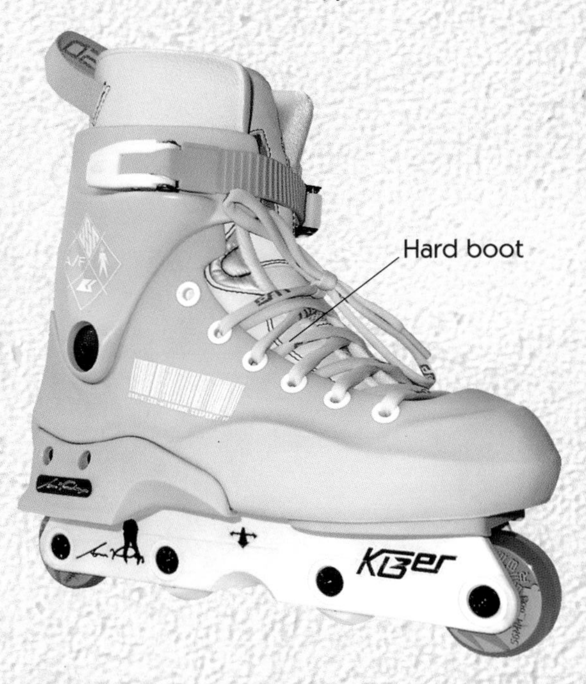

Hard Boots Hard boots have a hard plastic shell. They're very supportive and ideal for grinding tricks.

Soft Boots These boots are soft and flexible like sneakers. Their outside skeleton supports the ankle.

Hybrid Boots Hybrid boots have soft and hard areas. The hard areas offer support. The soft areas offer the flexibility needed to perform certain tricks.

Frames
The frame is attached to the underside of the boot and holds the wheels. All the major inline skate manufacturers have agreed on the same way of fitting boots to frames. So you can swap frames and wheels to customize your skates.

Inline skating involves a lot of falling down, especially when you're a beginner. It's impossible to avoid a few bumps and scrapes. That's why it's always a good idea to wear full safety equipment.

Falling and Getting Up Again

Experienced skaters can reach very high speeds. When accidents happen, there's often very little time to react. Your knees, elbows, wrists, and head are the most prone to injury. If you wear safety gear, you'll see your technique improve, because you won't be so nervous about falling. When you do fall, it's important to fall the right way.

GUIDE #2

HOW TO FALL

If you feel yourself losing balance, you should always try to control the fall. The shortest distance to fall is forward onto your knee pads with your hands in front of you. Bending your knees will soften the blow.

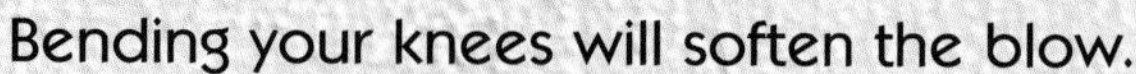

Falling Forward

Protect your face by taking some of the impact on your elbow pads.

Falling Backward

Twist around so that you're facing into the fall. Try not to trap your hands beneath you.

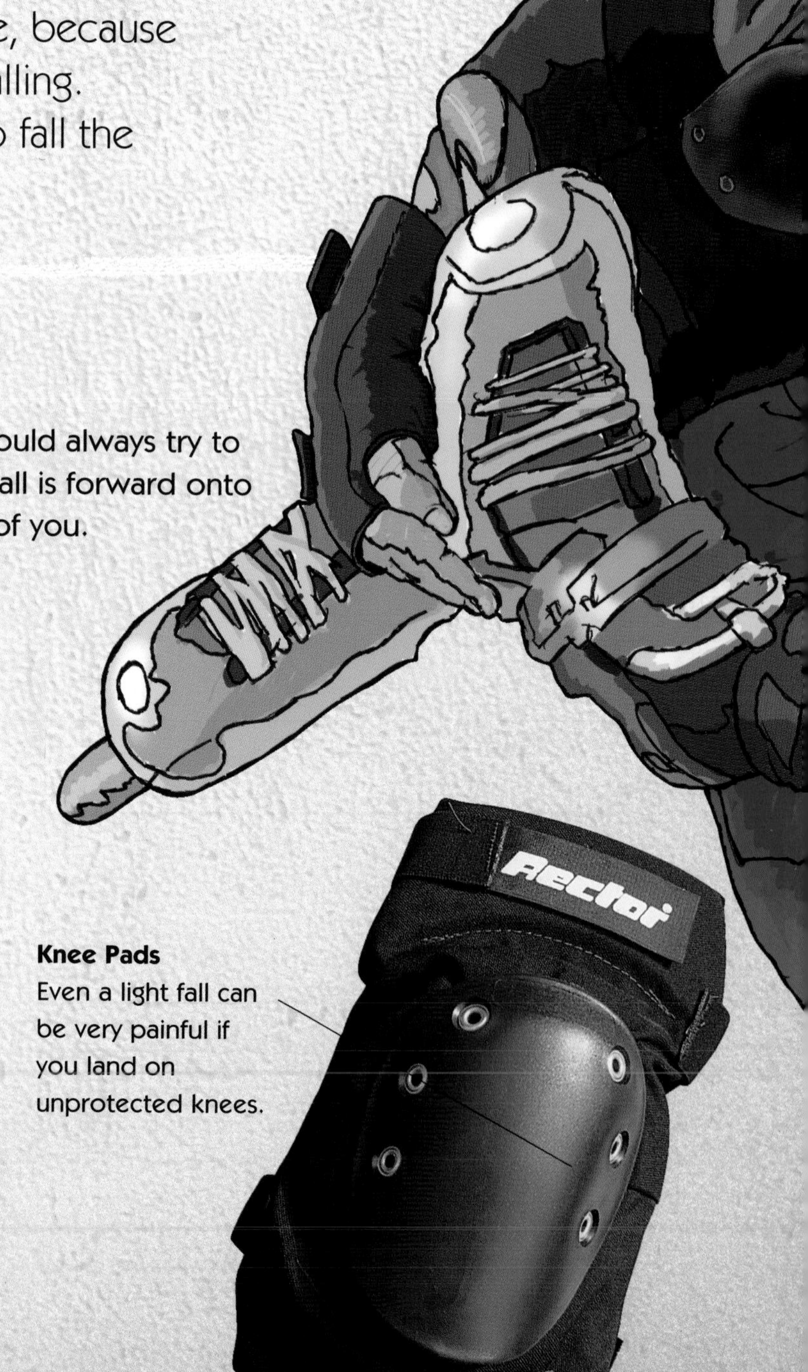

Knee Pads

Even a light fall can be very painful if you land on unprotected knees.

Helmet
It's important to choose a helmet that fits perfectly. Replace your helmet if it suffers a hard knock.
Wrist Guards
These have a solid plastic insert that absorbs the impact of a fall.
Elbow Pads
Your elbows are very prone to injury. These pads are adjusted with Velcro straps.
Rector
Gaskets
Vert skaters wear these under capped knee pads for extra protection.
SMITH

Getting Started

When you first put on a pair of skates, it feels very strange. But if you learn the basics of standing up and pushing off, you'll soon build up your confidence.

THE BASICS
Joining a beginners' class is a great way of learning the basics and meeting other skaters.

First Steps

It's important to feel comfortable just standing still on your blades. Start on a soft surface, like a carpet or a lawn, and practice keeping your balance. Then try walking around on your blades. You'll gradually get used to the feel of them. Next practice getting back on your feet after a fall—you'll probably need this!

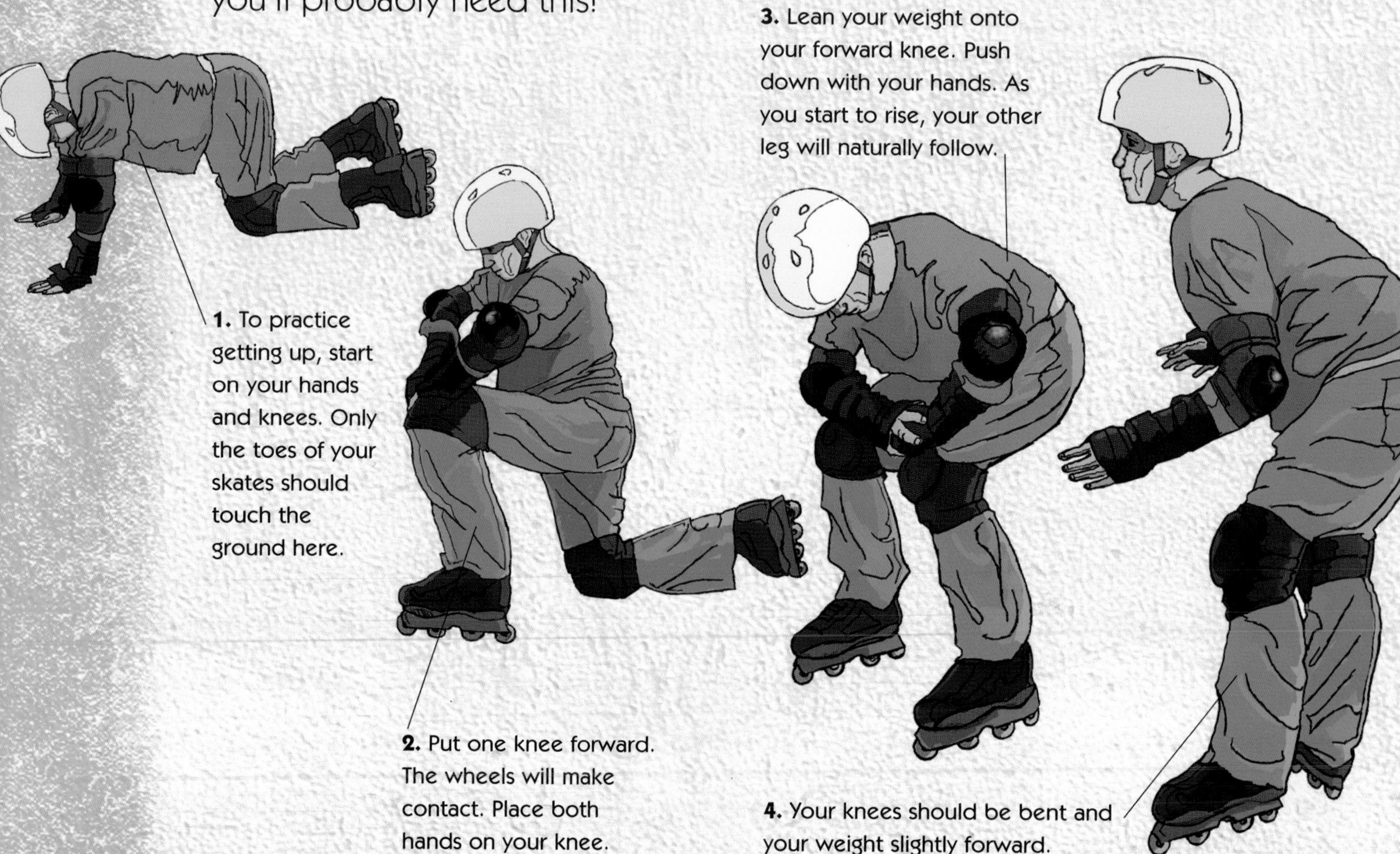

1. To practice getting up, start on your hands and knees. Only the toes of your skates should touch the ground here.

2. Put one knee forward. The wheels will make contact. Place both hands on your knee.

3. Lean your weight onto your forward knee. Push down with your hands. As you start to rise, your other leg will naturally follow.

4. Your knees should be bent and your weight slightly forward.

Pushing Off

Once you're confident that you can stay upright, you can start striding—gliding slowly without lifting up the wheels. To steer, position the front skate into the direction in which you want to travel and push forward with your rear skate.

1. With your knees bent, place your feet in a V shape. **2.** With your weight on your left skate, bring the right one in front of you. **3.** Push your left skate forward. **4.** Shift your weight onto your right skate. **5.** Build up your rhythm, always pushing with your rear skate.

HEEL BRAKE
It takes practice to use the heel brake efficiently, but it's the best way for beginners to stop.

Stopping

At first, you'll probably skate so slowly that you'll come to a halt if you stop stroking for a second. But when you do start moving faster and want to stop, don't slow down by leaning backward. You might fall backward and hurt your lower back—one of the most common and painful skating injuries. Instead stop by using your heel brake. Place that skate forward. Point your toe upward, and let the brake gently rub along the ground. Gradually add more pressure, and try to keep your balance.

GUIDE #3

A-FRAME TURN

This is the first way that most beginners learn to turn. The trick is knowing how to shift your weight from one skate to the other.

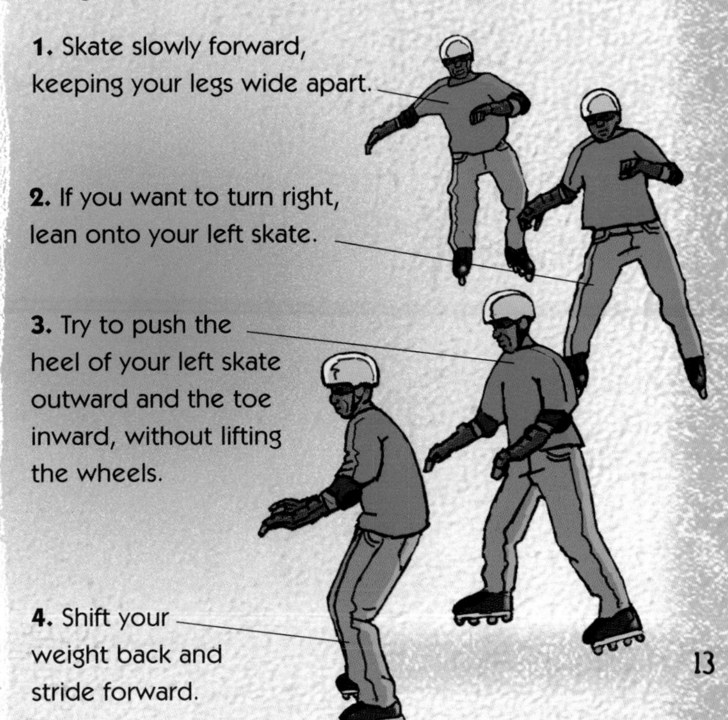

Once you're able to skate comfortably along a flat surface, it's time to learn a few tricks.

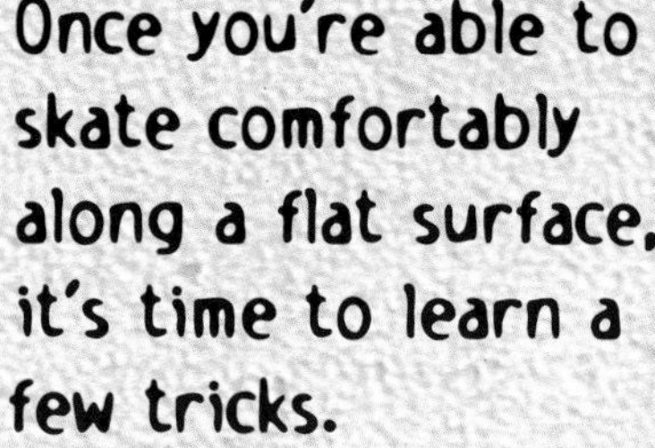

A BASIC JUMP

The most important part of any airborne trick is the landing. Before you even take off, you should check that you're not going to fall when you land.

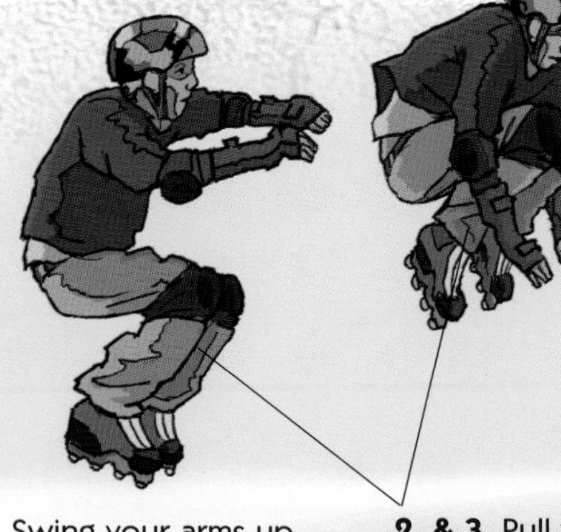

1. Swing your arms up to give you momentum to leave the ground.

2. & 3. Pull your knees against your chest for a faster and higher air.

4. Start to straighten out again as you reach the highest point of the air.

5. & 6. Keep your knees bent. Land with your weight forward and your legs apart.

Airs

In an "air," both your skates leave the ground. When skaters go off a ramp or jump down steps, they've caught some air. Performing a trick or a grab while doing an air looks more interesting.

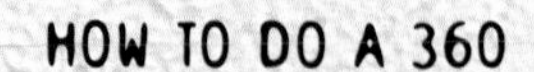

Spins

The name of a spin describes how many degrees you turn in the air. If you spin so that you're facing backward, it's a 180. Turning completely around is a 360. The biggest spin ever pulled on a pair of skates is a 1260—three and a half rotations.

HOW TO DO A 360

Using your arms for momentum, spin your upper body around as quickly as you can. Your lower half will follow. When you reach the top of the air, check where you're going to land. Bend your knees to absorb the impact.

STALL

1. Jump onto the obstacle when you're about one and a half feet (half a meter) away from it.
2. With knees bent, lock your skates onto the obstacle and balance with your arms.
3. Push yourself firmly away.

Stalls and Grinds

Stalling means jumping onto an obstacle, staying still for a few seconds, and then jumping off. The obstacle could be anything from a stair or a curb to the top edge of a ramp. Grinding means locking your skates (except the wheels) onto a surface and sliding down it. You need to know how to stall before you can grind.

CONCRETE WALL
Concrete is a great surface to grind.

Advanced Tricks

Only try advanced tricks if you are a skilled skater. To avoid injury, you should wear full safety equipment. With all tricks, it's important to start on small obstacles and gradually move on to bigger ones.

Flips and Inverts

Flips are backward or forward somersaults, where your whole body turns a complete circle. An invert is a handstand done in a half-pipe (a U-shaped ramp). To perform an invert, skate into a half-pipe. With some speed, skate up to the metal edge, or coping, at the top of the ramp. As your skates leave the ramp, bend over and plant your hands on the coping. Your lower half will keep moving upward. To get down, place your feet back on the ramp and push off with your hands at the same time.

INVERT

Once you've mastered the basic invert, you can hold the coping with one hand and pull a grab before you head back down.

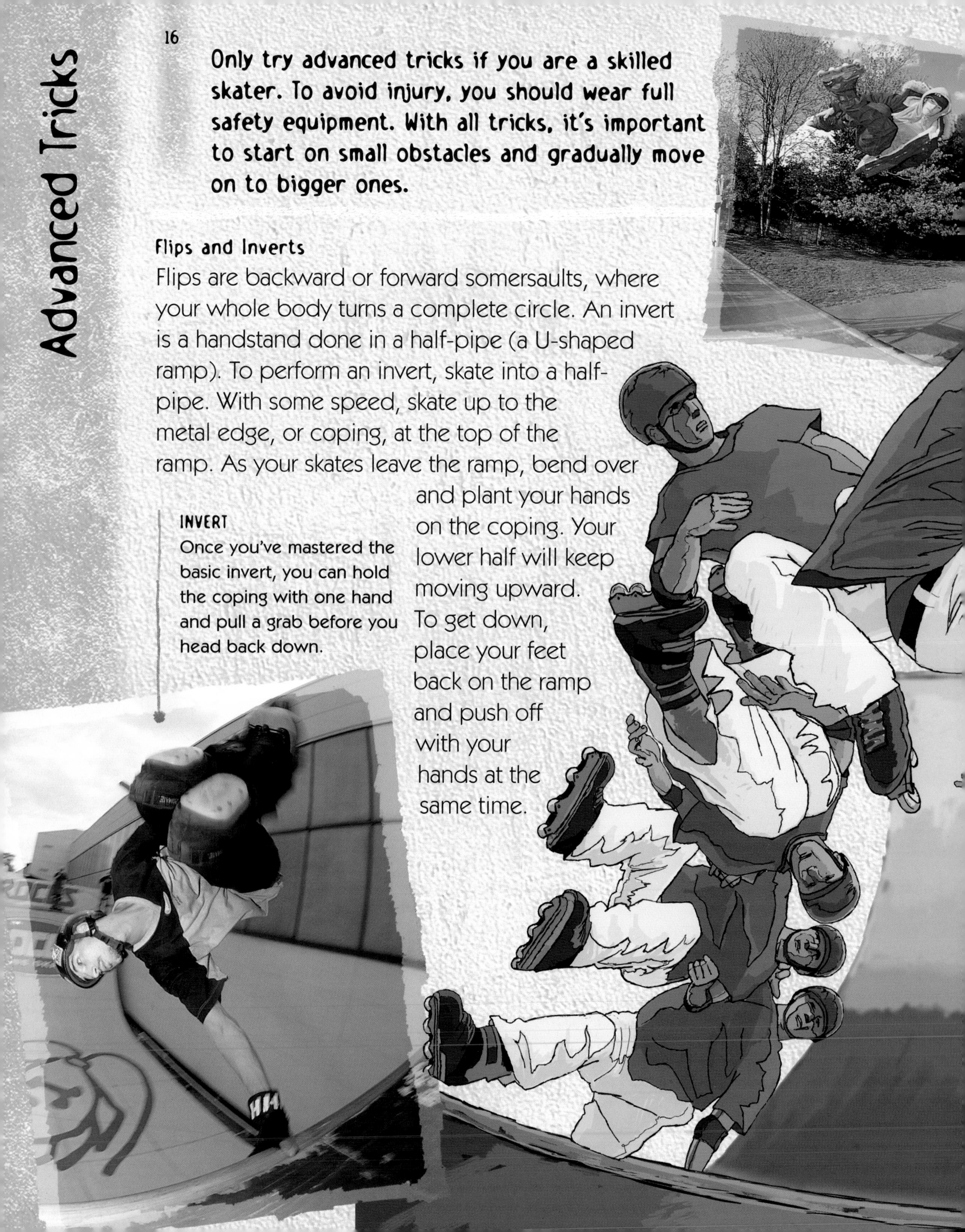

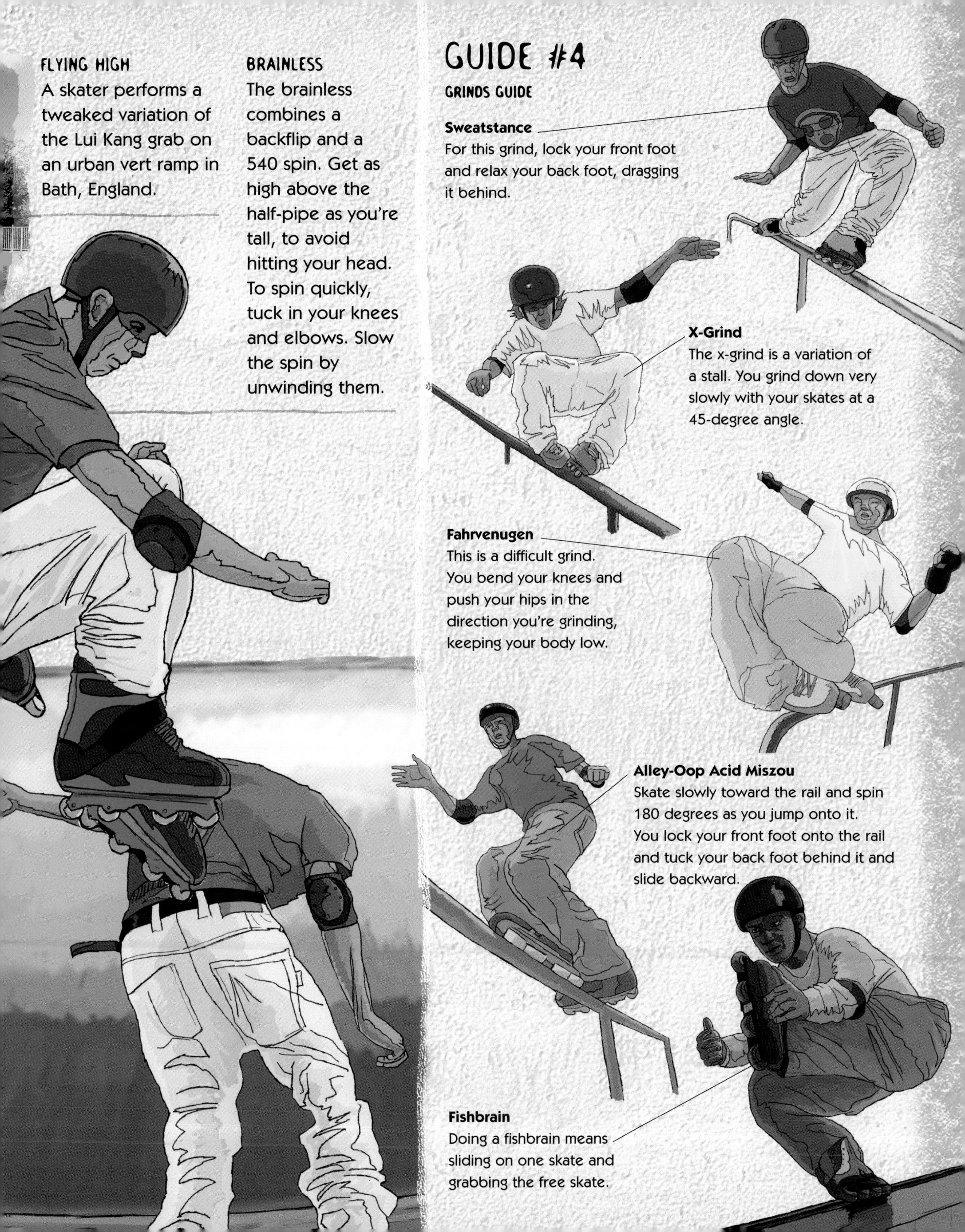

FLYING HIGH
A skater performs a tweaked variation of the Lui Kang grab on an urban vert ramp in Bath, England.

BRAINLESS
The brainless combines a backflip and a 540 spin. Get as high above the half-pipe as you're tall, to avoid hitting your head. To spin quickly, tuck in your knees and elbows. Slow the spin by unwinding them.

GUIDE #4

GRINDS GUIDE

Sweatstance
For this grind, lock your front foot and relax your back foot, dragging it behind.

X-Grind
The x-grind is a variation of a stall. You grind down very slowly with your skates at a 45-degree angle.

Fahrvenugen
This is a difficult grind. You bend your knees and push your hips in the direction you're grinding, keeping your body low.

Alley-Oop Acid Miszou
Skate slowly toward the rail and spin 180 degrees as you jump onto it. You lock your front foot onto the rail and tuck your back foot behind it and slide backward.

Fishbrain
Doing a fishbrain means sliding on one skate and grabbing the free skate.

In the early days of inline skating, people simply rolled. Modern "aggressive" skating is divided into three styles—street, skatepark, and vert.

Street Skating

The idea of street skating is to conquer the streets and test yourself on its obstacles. Handrails, steps, and ledges make up the skater's urban playground. Skaters have to be aware of dangers, such as cars and other people. If a skater, riding at full speed, collides with someone, the results can be fatal. It's crucial that you respect those around you. Skating may be banned in areas where skaters become a nuisance.

STREET GRIND
A skater grinds down a handrail at an apartment building.

Vert Skating

Vert ramps are usually found in skateparks. They're a type of half-pipe. The sides of the ramp become vertical walls. They launch you into the air so you can perform spectacular stunts. Vert ramps are about 10 feet (3 meters) high and 26 feet (8 meters) wide. It takes a lot of skill, practice, and courage to tackle a vert ramp. Vert skating is probably the most eye-catching discipline in the sport.

INVERT GRAB
A skater performs an invert grab on a vert ramp.

Skatepark

Skateparks exist in many towns and cities. You'll see skateboarders, BMX riders, and inline skaters. The parks themselves range in size from small outdoor facilities to huge indoor parks. Skateparks have specially made ramps and obstacles to challenge you. The larger parks employ trained staff who can advise you on your skating and even teach you a few new tricks.

SKATEPARK GRIND
As well as ramps, skateparks have many of the obstacles you find on the street, such as this railing.

Street skating is the original form of aggressive skating. Skaters used to search the streets looking for obstacles, like steps to jump and hills to speed down.

New Challenges

Skates with four large wheels weren't up to the job of sliding and grinding. The wheels stuck to any surface. The answer was the "anti-rockered" wheel system—two small, hard wheels in the middle of the setup. The wheels were raised slightly so the skater could lock onto grinds and turn easily.

ALLEY-OOP
Using the large gap between the middle wheels, this skater performs an alley-oop (backward) grind.

Using the Terrain

With the invention of the anti-rockered system, aggressive skating was born. Street skaters could go after any obstacle on the street, from rails and ledges to walls and curbs. Skateparks mimic many of these street obstacles, and there's no danger to pedestrians (people on foot) or traffic.

HANDRAIL GRIND
Simon Coburn demonstrates a fahrvenugen down a handrail.

LEDGE GRIND
A squared-off ledge is just as challenging as a narrow handrail.

ROOF JUMP
Anti-rockered skates turn easily. This means that skaters can do stunts and airs like this roof jump.

A vert ramp is similar to a half-pipe. Both of them curve upward on both sides. Unlike on a half-pipe, the curves on a vert ramp reach a vertical angle.

Grinds and Spins

Spectacular inline stunts are possible on a vert ramp. Vert ramps allow skaters to perform higher airs and do many spins. You should know how to do a 180 and skate backward before you try vert riding. Start skating from the flat bottom and not from the top! Inexperienced skaters can be seriously injured by dropping into a ramp. Vert skaters nearly always wear full protection.

VERT GRAB
A skater does a flatspin—a spin in a horizontal position—on a vert ramp.

BOTTOM AND TRANSITION
Half-pipes and vert ramps are usually made of wood. The horizontal surface is called the flat bottom. The curved arc is the transition.

Vert Doubles

Vert ramps are often used for demonstrations at large shows. Skaters thrill crowds by flying over 13 feet (4 meters) in the air. In some vert skating competitions, skaters compete in pairs on the ramps at the same time. These are called vert doubles events. Skaters spin and grind over and under each other during their runs. This is a very exciting but dangerous competition.

VERT AIR
Vert ramps are usually 10 feet (3 meters) high. Add a 6-foot air and you're a long way up!

GUIDE #5

GRABS GUIDE

Once you've started to catch some air, try one of these grabs.

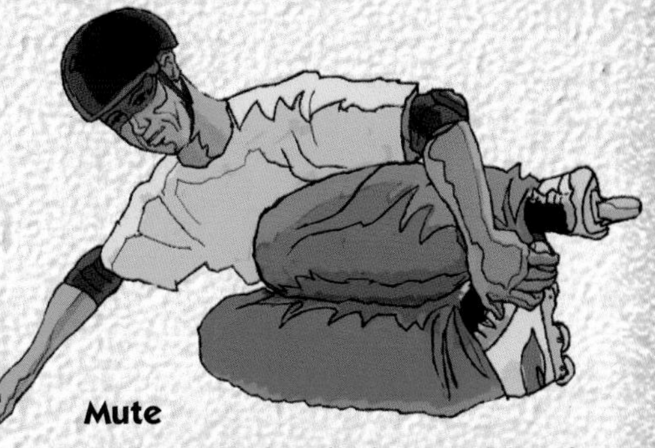

Mute
Tuck up and grab the outside of your opposite boot.

Safety
Your arm grabs the boot on the same side, with your legs tucked up.

Lui Kang
Tuck one leg up and grab the boot, extending the other leg.

Parallel
Reach right across your body and grab the opposite skate.

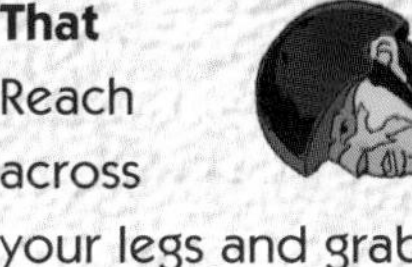

That
Reach across your legs and grab the frame of the opposite boot.

In the 1970s, skaters did tricks in empty backyard swimming pools. Soon concrete skateparks were built for public use.

THE OLD DAYS
The ancestors of modern skateparks were crudely-constructed concrete ramps in parks.

Changing Fashions

In the early 1980s, many concrete parks closed. Skaters built their own curved wooden ramps. They used tubing as edging on the ramps, so skaters could grind at the top. They grouped other obstacles together. The modern plywood skatepark was born. Many towns and cities have indoor skateparks, so you can use them year-round.

FUN FACTORY
Skateparks have ramps of different sizes for skaters of all abilities. Never rest on an obstacle. Other skaters might collide with you.

QUARTER-BOWL
A skater grinds the coping of a quarter-bowl (a huge skatepark ramp).

What to Expect

As well as ramps, skateparks usually have rails and ledges similar to those on the street. Without any cars or pedestrians in sight, riding these obstacles is a lot safer! Skateparks often have rules and etiquette to keep them safe. That way every skater knows when and where they can ride. It's worth learning about this information before you skate.

MISTRAL

A skater demonstrates a mistral grind, edging down a rail very slowly.

GUIDE #6

RAMPS GUIDE

These are examples of the most popular ramps.

Quarter-pipe

A quarter-pipe is a ramp that looks like a pipe cut into fourths.

Half-pipe

Not surprisingly, a half-pipe is twice the size of a quarter-pipe. It has a sloping arc.

Full-pipe

A full-pipe is a completely circular wall. Some professional skaters can skate upside down on a full-pipe!

Hip

A hip consists of two gently curving slopes with a sharp ridge between them.

Spine

The spine is a narrow ledge dividing two quarter-pipes.

Inline skating is a naturally competitive sport. Skaters want to test themselves and impress others. Organized competitions are popular, too.

VERT RAMP
Professional skater Fabiola Da Silva catches some air above a vert ramp.

Three Events

Just as there are three main styles of skating, there are also three main events—street, vert, and real street. Each one is a test of style, creativity, difficulty, and consistency.

Competitions take place in skateparks, on specially built courses, on vert ramps, or even on the street.

RAIL GRIND
The obstacles in street competitions resemble those of a real street.

Street Competition

Despite its name, a street competition takes place in a skatepark. Skaters grind obstacles such as ramps, rails, quarter-pipes, and boxes. Competitors have two one-minute runs. On each run, they try to make as many points as possible out of a total of 100. The judges are experienced skaters, who know all the latest moves and how many points each one deserves.

Vert Competition

These take place on a vert ramp. Skaters have two-minute runs to use the ramp to the best of their ability. They have to combine grinds, airs, and spins. Extra points are awarded for tricks performed well above the coping.

SKATEPARK STALL
A skater stalls on one of the safety barriers in a skatepark-based street contest.

Real Street Competitions

This is the latest type of competition. Skaters use a real street as their competition arena. Specially invited skaters start on small obstacles and try to pull better tricks than the contestant before them. It works by way of elimination. The best skaters qualify to go through to the next round on a bigger obstacle.

ZIGZAG
With gravity on their side, plenty of aggressive skaters can grind straight rails. Not many can cope with the horizontal sections. These sorts of rails are called "kink" rails.

It takes a lot of hard work to become a professional skater. These experts earn a living by advertising equipment made by particular companies and from prize money.

JOSH PETTY
Josh autographs a fan's T-shirt during one of his many promotional tours.

Street Stars

Most new tricks are based on street skating. So, skate companies are always on the lookout for creative and original street skaters. Street stars travel the world. They skate in competitions and demonstrations in skateparks and on the street.

Josh Petty

Josh Petty is from Santee, California, and is known as the wild child of aggressive skating. His fast and furious style always includes the latest tricks. He is sponsored by some of the top makers of skates, wheels, and clothing.

Billy Prislin

Billy Prislin is one of the best street skaters. He is part of the International Senate Clothing and Salomon Skate teams.

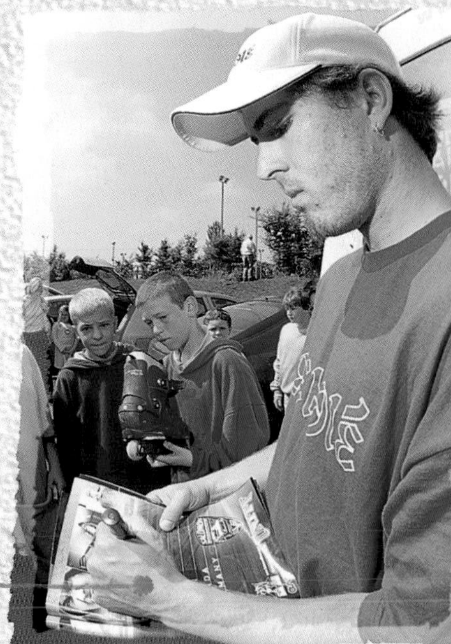

BILLY PRISLIN
Billy Prislin has recently traveled all over the world on the famous Salomon Safari Tour.

AARON FEINBERG
A star of videos and magazines, Aaron won a gold medal at the X Games on his sixteenth birthday. He is a seasoned competition skater and street-skating hero.

Vert Stars

Vert skaters are highly respected within the sport. It takes a lot of skill and technique to tackle a vert ramp, let alone to become a professional vert skater. As a result, there are fewer vert skaters than street skaters.

CESAR MORA

Cesar Mora was born in Spain but has lived in Sydney, Australia, for most of his life. He has been a professional vert skater for many years.

FABIOLA DA SILVA

"Fabby" was born in Sao Paulo, Brazil. One of the top stars of vert skating, she mainly competes against men.

GUIDE #7

THE PRO-SKATING LIFE

Many people aspire to be professional skaters, but it isn't a carefree life. Pro skaters have responsibilities to their sponsors. They perform demonstrations at public events and trade shows. They also have to skate for photo shoots for advertising and magazines. They may also have to tour for weeks at a time to promote their sponsors.

On skate tours, companies often give out free samples of their products.

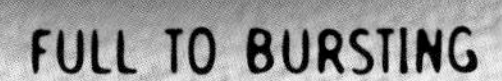

FULL TO BURSTING

Life on the tour bus can be cramped and uncomfortable. It's not just skaters who have to fit in the bus, it's their luggage, too.

FURTHER READING

Bizley, Kirk. *Inline Skating.* Chicago: Heinemann Library, 2000.

Dugard, Martin. *In-line Skating Made Easy.* Old Saybrook, CT: Globe Pequot Press, 1996.

Edwards, Chris. *The Young Inline Skater.* New York: DK Publishing, 1996.

Gedatus, Gustav Mark. *In-line Skating for Fitness.* Mankato, MN: LifeMatters, 2001.

Kaminker, Laura. *In-line Skating!* New York: Rosen Publishing Group, 1999.

Maurer, Tracy Nelson. *In-line Skating.* Vero Beach, FL: Rourke Publishing, 2002.

Millar, Cam. *In-line Skating Basics.* New York: Sterling Publishing Company, 1996.

Miller, Liz. *Get Rolling.* Camden, ME: Ragged Mountain Press, 1998.

Nealy, William. *Inline!* Birmingham, AL: Menasha Ridge Press, 1998.

Rappelfeld, Joel. *The Complete In-line Skater.* New York: St. Martin's Press, 1996.

Terry, Russell J. *Fixing and Skating with In-line and Roller Skates.* New York: Vantage Press, 1997.

Werner, Doug. *In-line Skater's Start-up.* San Diego, CA: Tracks Publishing, 1995.

Witt, Alexa. *It's Great to Skate!* New York: Simon & Schuster, 2000.

WEBSITES

Aggressive.com
<http://www.aggressive.com/>

Daily Bread Magazine
<http://www.dbmag.com/index.htm>

Gain Presence.com
<http://www.how2sk8.com/gpallphp/>

Inline Online (spanish-language site)
<http://www.inlineonline.com/>

Irish Rolling
<http://www.irishrolling.com/>

Pure-Skate.com
<http://www.pure-skate.com/>

Roces
<http://www.roces.com>

Rollerblade
<http://www.rollerblade.com>

Salomon
<http://aggressive.salomoninline.com/others/home.asp>

Skategirls.net
<http://www.skategirls.net/>

Totalskate.com
<http://www.totalskate.com/>

Unity Magazine
<http://www.unitymag.com/>

All the Internet addresses (URLs) given in this book were valid at the time of going to press. However, due to the dynamic nature of the Internet, some addresses and content may have changed, or sites may have ceased to exist since publication. While the author and publishers regret any inconvenience this may cause readers, no responsibility for any such changes can be accepted by either the author or the publishers.

Glossary

aggressive: performing skating stunts, grinds, and stalls on obstacles, such as rails, walls, and ramps

air: to launch into the air or leave the skating surface

anti-rocker: a type of wheel setup that has small wheels in the middle of the skate and larger wheels on the outside. This setup allows for easier grinding.

bearings: the mechanisms inside the middle of each wheel that make the wheel turn with less friction

coping: a metal tube at the top of a ramp on which skaters grind or stall

discipline: a particular style of skating, such as street, skatepark, or vert

dropping in: entering a ramp from the platforms at the top of it

durometer: the measure of a wheel's hardness. Harder wheels have a higher durometer reading and are better for grinding. The lowest durometer reading is 74a, and the highest is 101a.

elimination: the process of getting rid of entrants in a skate competition, one by one, until there is a clear winner

endorsing: supporting. Professional skaters endorse brands of skate in return for payment.

fakie: doing a trick backward

grind: to force your skates along a hard edge

grommet: a nickname for a young skater

half-pipe: a U-shaped ramp with two curved (transitioned) walls. Many different variations and sizes exist. A quarter-pipe is half the size of a half-pipe.

invert: any upside-down air

maneuver: a move

momentum: the force of a moving object

setup: a particular way a skate or its wheels are arranged for different types of skating

stall: a trick that involves momentarily stopping before pulling out of a move. Stalls are performed on the coping of a ramp, a rail, or a ledge.

transition: the curved arc of a ramp

vert ramp: a curved ramp, sometimes over 13 feet (4 meters) tall, with a transition that reaches a vertical angle

X Games: a massive annual competition held all over the United States. It features all extreme sports, such as mountain biking, skateboarding, BMX, and inline skating.

Index